"This book is dedicated to my parents, who taught me the value of reading (and writing), and to the next generation - who I hope will stay forever curious."

- Christopher Mitchell

First Edition, 2023
TRAVEL THE WORLD AROUND YOU!
© 2023 by Christopher Mitchell
All rights reserved.

No part of this book may be reproduced, stored, or transmitted without permission from the author or publisher.

Created in collaboration with Timmy Bauer
Produced and Published by Dinosaur House
Edited by Bri Mitchell
Art by Dinosaur House, a kids book production studio
Lead Artist: Alejandra Moreno

www.DinosaurHouse.com

TRAVEL THE WORLD AROUND YOU!

By Christopher Mitchell

Theo's classmates are talking about their plans for the upcoming school break.

Nora is going to a fancy hotel in Aruba, Sophia is visiting her nana in Montreal, Quebec. Joseph is going back to his favourite ride in Orlando, Florida, and Taylor is going on a safari in Tanzania.

Theo is feeling disappointed. He's happy for his classmates, but he is staying home for the break.

He just moved here, and he doesn't know what he's going to do for the break. He doesn't even have any favourite spots to visit in town.

TRAVEL SCHOLARSHIP CONTEST!

One lucky student and a parent will win a **FREE** trip to Europe. Get a stamp on your "passport" by a local professional in the following subjects:

- SCIENCE
- MATH
- SPANISH
- LANGUAGE ARTS
- HISTORY
- MUSIC

Tell us everything you learn in an essay. The student with the most interesting paper will win the travel scholarship!

A travel scholarship? This could be Theo's chance!
Do you think Theo should enter the contest?

After school, Theo comes home to his best friend, his wise and silly cat named Kotu.

He tells Kotu all about the contest, and they spend the whole afternoon brainstorming where to get the passport stamped!

"I love travelling! If our mom and dad never travelled to Turkey, they never would have found me! I would still be on the streets of Istanbul, fishing for my next meal."

Can you guess which stamps they will get here?

After dinner, the Chef gives Theo's passport a big red STAMP!

The next morning, Theo and Kotu go to the library. They learn how to check out a book, and they each get their own library card.

At the end of their visit, they get their Language Arts stamp!

Later that day, Theo and Kotu go grocery shopping with their parents. Theo is frustrated that he can't find any math professionals in his town. He doesn't even know where to look.

CHECK OUT

Theo gives the correct amount to the cashier and gets a stamp from his mom!

Counting your total at the grocery store is one way to use math every day.

Can you think of any other ways you use math?

The day to deliver the stamps and essay arrives. Theo has worked really hard, and is proud of his work.

I've been exploring new places, trying new things, and enjoying the world around me. I have been travelling this whole time, and I never even left my town!

Do you think Theo's paper will win the contest?

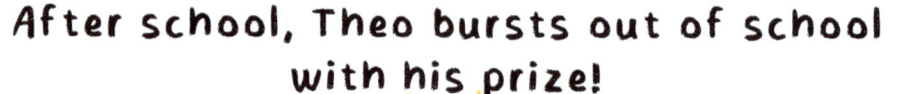

After school, Theo bursts out of school with his prize!

THEO WON!

FRANCE AND ITALY TRIP WINNER!

Embracing his inner curiosity opened Theo up to a whole new sense of meaning in the world around him.

Now that he has found that, he can't wait to explore a whole new continent, and then more of this wonderful world.

THE END.

LET'S TALK ABOUT THE STORY!

01. HOW FAR AWAY DO YOU HAVE TO GO FOR IT TO BE CONSIDERED TRAVELLING?

[A] One Hundred Kilometers
[B] Three Thousand Kilometers
[C] Even in your own town or city, as long as you have the travelling mindset!

02. WHICH OF THESE THINGS DID THEO AND KOTU LEARN IN THEIR TRAVELS?

[A] How to plant a garden
[B] How to read music
[C] How to move a couch

03. DISCUSSION: What are some places in your town, city, or community that you'd like to travel to and why?

Get FREE coloring pages from this book
SCAN the code below with your smartphone!

Published by

DINOSAUR HOUSE

www.DinosaurHouse.com/books

www.ingramcontent.com/pod-product-compliance
Lightning Source LLC
Chambersburg PA
CBHW041406010526
44107CB00015B/1093